BASS DRUM CONTROL SOLOS

by Colin Bailey

Also by Colin Bailey:

BASS DRUM CONTROL
DRUM SOLOS: THE ART OF PHRASING

ISBN 0-634-04950-X

HAL•LEONARD® CORPORATION

7777 W. BLUEMOUND RD. P.O. BOX 13819 MILWAUKEE, WI 53213

In Australia contact:
Hal Leonard Australia Pty. Ltd.
22 Taunton Drive P.O. Box 5130
Cheltenham East, 3192 Victoria, Australia
Email: ausadmin@halleonard.com

Visit Hal Leonard Online at
www.halleonard.com

PREFACE

I wrote this book as a follow up to the original BASS DRUM CONTROL. The material here is in solo form, utilising Toms and Cymbals along with the Snare and Bass Drum. This is the way I use the Bass Drum in my soloing, extensively, as it is after all, one of the Drums in the set along with the Snare and Toms and I feel it should be played as such. It can add so much to the overall sound of the Drum set, and present more options in what can be played. By adding groups of two, three, four or more Bass Drum beats to solos, it will expand your solo vocabulary immensely. I hope that this book will encourage Drummers to use the Bass Drum more when soloing.

All of this material can be played on a single or double pedal.

TEMPOS

The tempo for any of the solos is wherever it feels comfortable to play them accurately and in time. Obviously, the more Bass Drum beats that there are in a group may slow down the tempo, because it's easier to play two or three beats than seven or eight. However, most of the solos sound better when played at a faster tempo.

NOTATION

I wrote these solos in sixteenth note patterns as I did in Bass Drum Control, using two staves, two bars each, for a four bar solo. Triplets are written the same. Any solo played as eighth notes will double the duration of any sixteenth note solo.

STICKING

I have written sticking which will be helpful in playing the solos where it's not an obvious R-L situation. In both endurance exercises I like to play all snare drum beats with either the right or left hand, not R-L. They are also both playable as R-L, whichever you are comfortable with.

ADAPTING TO A FOUR PIECE SET

The idea of course, is to replace the missing mid-tom with the snare or low-tom.
A good example of this is in the first solo on page four. It would sound good to use the low-tom in that situation. In solo number two on page four, also low-tom. In solo number three I would use the snare as the replacement, so that you have hi- tom, snare and low-tom in the first and third bars. Solo number four would be the same as solo number two. It's not difficult to figure out how to substitute for the mid-tom.

COMING OUT OF A SOLO

It is very important to know what to play on the first beat after a solo, whether you are going back into time or playing a beat to finish the solo, not in a time playing context.
There's a rule of thumb that if the last beat of the solo is on a high end Drum, snare or toms, the first beat of the next bar or the end of exercise solo, would be cymbal and Bass Drum. If the last beat of the solo is Bass Drum, then you would play cymbal and snare. This applies most of the time. Occasionally it may feel right to play two Bass Drum beats as the last beat of a solo and first beat of time.

PLAYING CYMBAL AND BASS DRUM TOGETHER

In these solos, play the cymbal and Bass Drum louder than the left-hand snare beats. It has a better effect than playing both at the same volume.

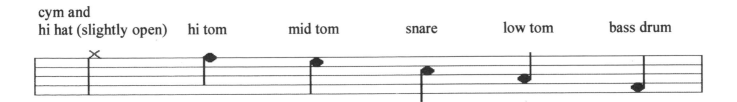

This will be the Ledger line note set-up throughout the Book

FOUR BAR SOLOS
1 and 2 BASS DRUM BEATS

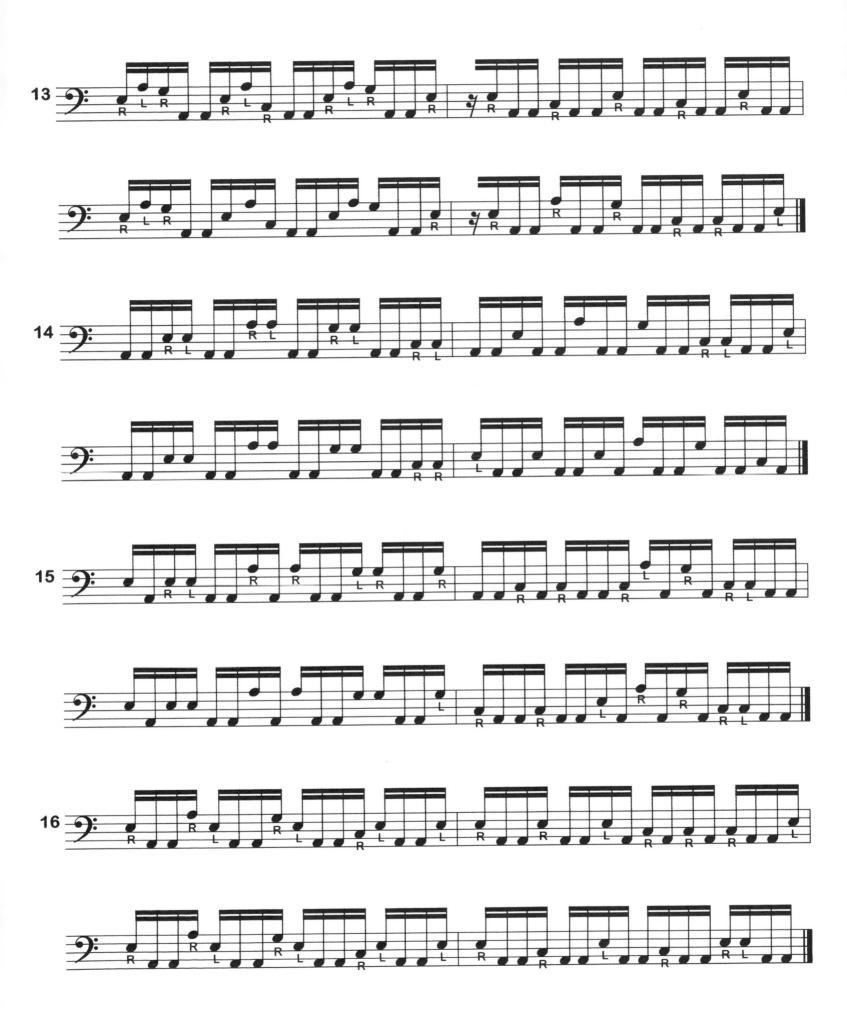

FOUR BAR SOLOS
1 and 2 BASS DRUM BEATS with CYMBAL

1 and 2 BASS DRUM BEATS with HI - HAT (Slightly Open)

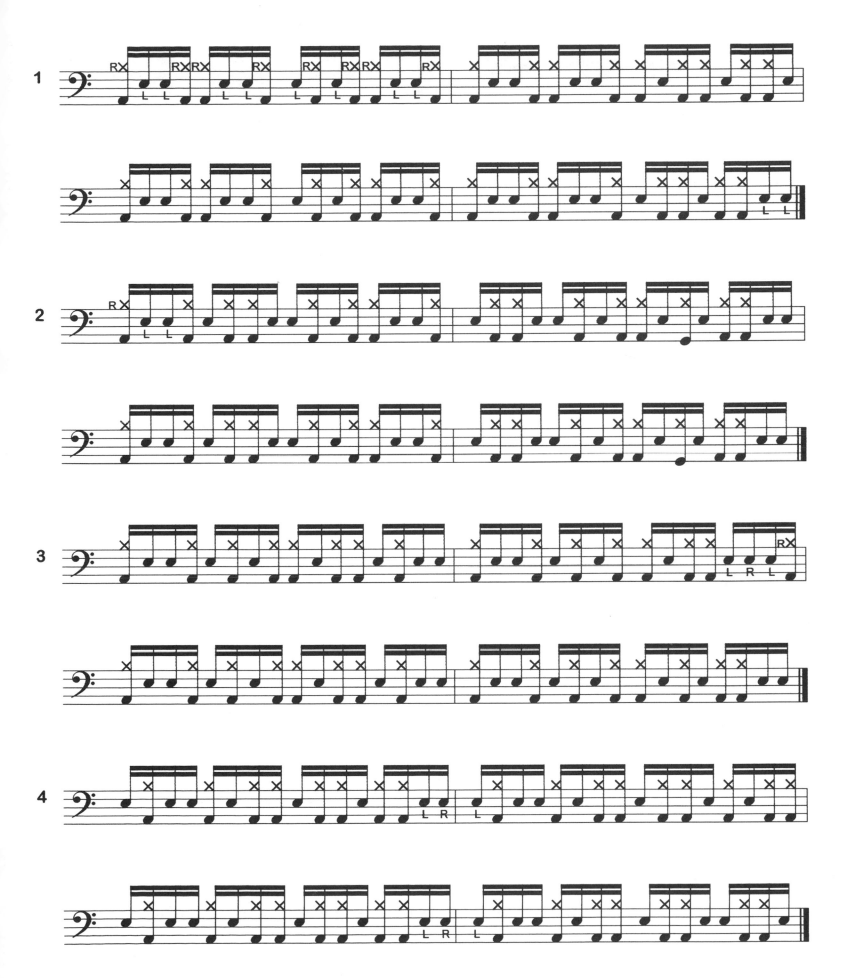

FOUR BAR SOLOS
1 - 2 and 3 BASS DRUM BEATS

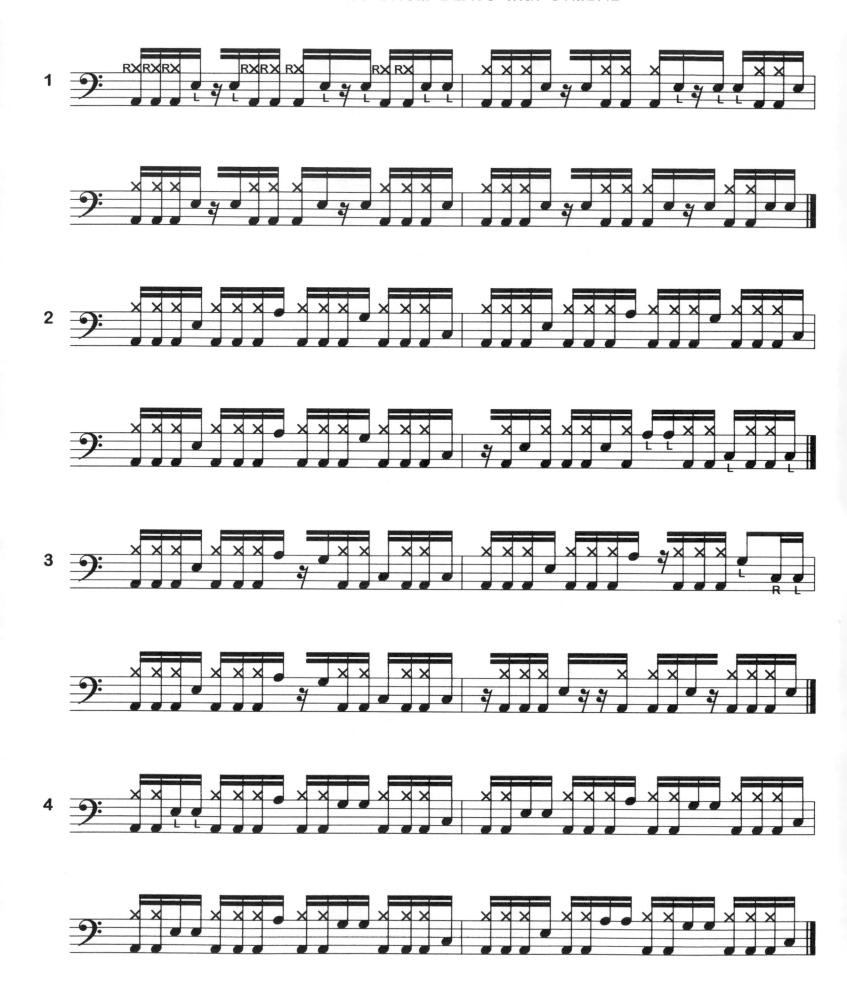

1 - 2 and 3 BASS DRUM BEATS with CYMBAL

FOUR BAR SOLOS

1 - 2 - 3 and 4 BASS DRUM BEATS

16

18

1 - 2 - 3 and 4 BASS DRUM BEATS with CYMBAL

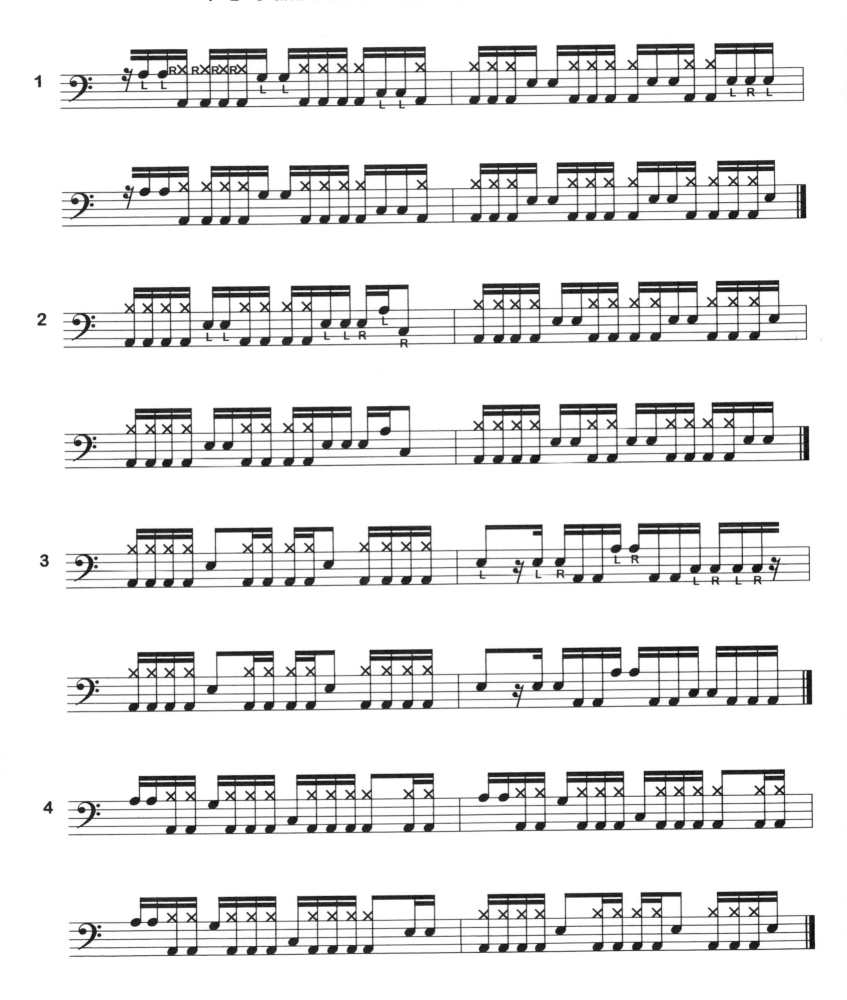

FOUR BAR SOLOS
1 to 5 BASS DRUM BEATS

1 to 6 BASS DRUM BEATS

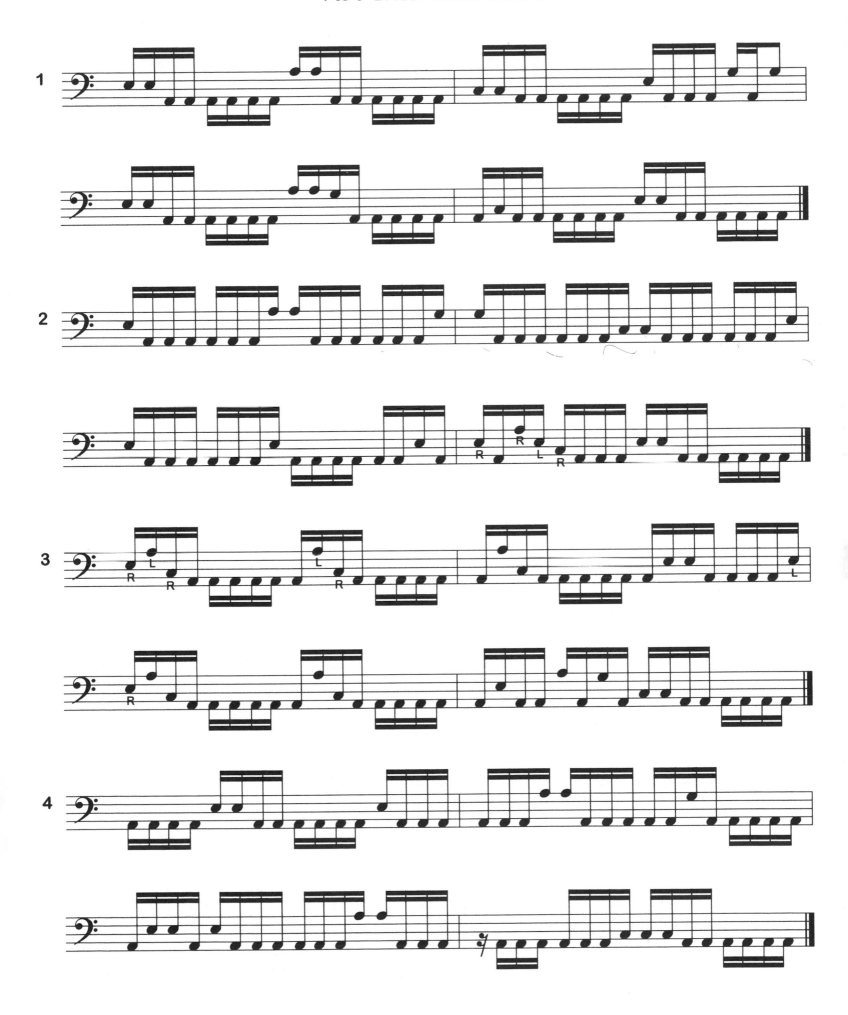

1 to 7 BASS DRUM BEATS

1 to 8 BASS DRUM BEATS

ENDURANCE EXERCISE
FROM 4 to 14 BASS DRUM BEATS

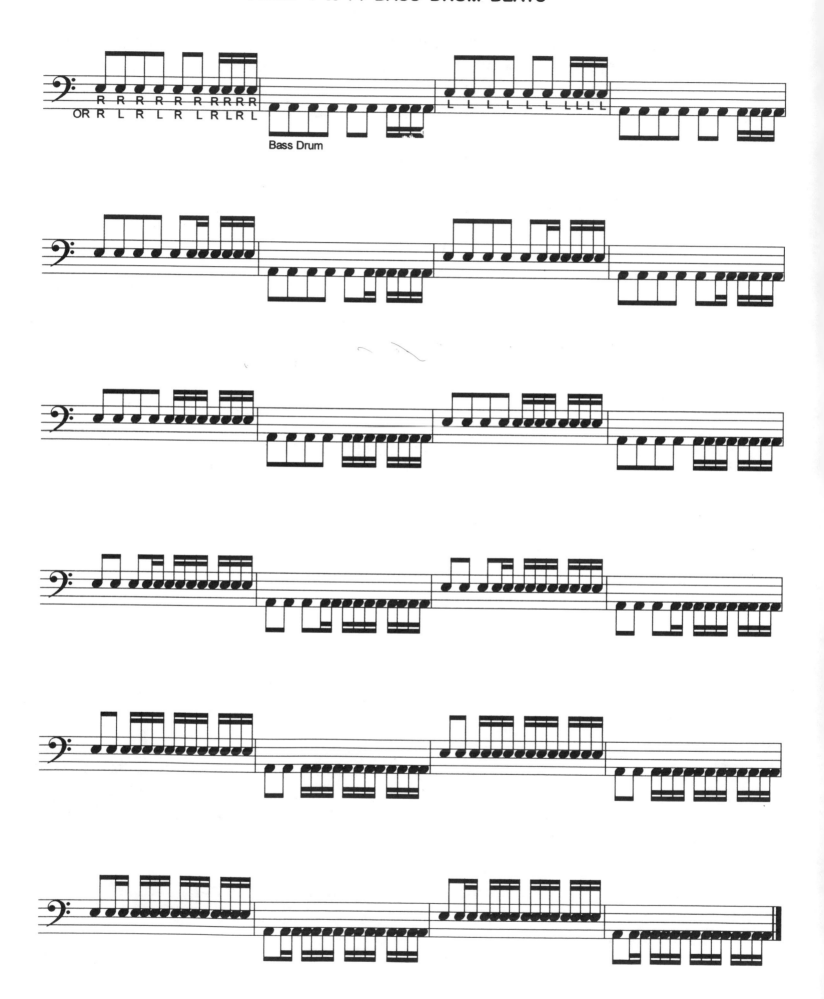

FOUR BAR SOLOS - TRIPLETS

26

28

TRIPLET 4's with CYMBAL

TRIPLET ENDURANCE EXERCISE
FROM 3 to 10 BASS DRUM BEATS

CD Track Index